HOW TO QUIT
FAST FASHION

100 EXPERT TIPS FOR
A SUSTAINABLE WARDROBE

EMMA MATHEWS
FOUNDER OF ETHICAL BRAND SOCKO

WELBECK

With thanks to the supportive and inspiring community built by the London Writers' Salon.

Published in 2020 by Welbeck
An imprint of the Welbeck Publishing Group
20 Mortimer Street
London W1T 3JW

A CIP catalogue for this book is available from the British Library.

ISBN 978-1-78739-506-0

Printed in China

10 9 8 7 6 5 4 3 2 1

CONTENTS

INTRODUCTION

The average person buys 60% more clothes and keeps them for half as long as they did 15 years ago, according to a Greenpeace report. But many people are now examining their shopping behaviours and waking up to the indefensible practices of fast fashion.

If you are one of these people, you've come to the right place to discover how to transform your concerns into actions. Between these pages, you will find tips that will help you to build a more sustainable relationship with your clothes and take control as a consumer in order to curb the impact your fashion choices have on our planet, and on the people working throughout the supply chain. In other words, they will show you how to quit fast fashion and embrace slow fashion.

Slow fashion values the craft that goes into our clothes. It repositions each garment from a throwaway commodity to an item to be treasured. It takes lessons from before this time of fast fashion and questions whether the convenient choice is always the best choice.

This book is not about discarding the clothes you have and starting again. Far from it. And it's not designed to guilt-trip you into making a change; the stark reality is out there and the fact that you're reading this means you're already aware of the devastating consequences of fast fashion. Instead, it gives you practical guidance on how you can actually have fun with fashion by doing more with less. It may even help you to unlock your true style along the way.

We start by exploring the relationship you have with your wardrobe and ways you can get the best use out of the clothes you already own. Then get some inspiration on ways you can upcycle the items that no longer serve your purpose. After getting crafty, we go into ways you can stay on trend by knowing and embracing your style and discovering alternatives to the big-name chains on the high street. Find out how to shop effectively, taking the power into your own hands to make more informed decisions when you shop. Finally, we look at ways you can extend the life of your clothes by giving them the correct care, from washing to mending and everything in between.

Consider this a line in the sand. A conscious decision to do things differently from now on. It's time to reconnect you with your clothes, and this book provides you with 100 tips on how to do just that. Let's get started!

RETHINKING YOUR WARDROBE

Taking the decision to ditch fast fashion doesn't mean starting over. Instead, it's a chance to draw a line in the sand and to make more conscious, intentional choices going forward. You can put yourself in a much stronger position next time the sale rail beckons by understanding your decision-making behaviours when it comes to selecting what to wear and getting a clearer idea of how you want to express yourself through your style. We start by paring your wardrobe down. Let's take a look at what you already own to decide what served a purpose in the past and what you want to take into your fast-fashion-free future.

#1
GO FOR QUALITY, NOT QUANTITY

Investing in one excellent item that you wear time and time again is worth so much more than having a selection of okay things to choose from. This is the most important principle of slow fashion, reflecting all the ethics of the movement. Choosing quality does not necessarily mean spending silly money, but it does mean selecting pieces that will last both physically and within your style. We'll go into this point in more detail in Chapter 4: Shopping More Efficiently, but bear it in mind when sorting through the clothes you already own.

#2
DO I WEAR THIS?

Analyzing your wardrobe requires a level of honesty that can be uncomfortable. Nobody said that quitting the habit of a lifetime was going to be easy – but it can be fun and will lead to a much more satisfying relationship with clothes and style. Whether you're getting ready, planning an outfit or sorting through your wardrobe, this is the first question to ask yourself.

Many of us keep items for sentimental reasons, or because we'll fit into it again one day. It may also be a great colour or design but doesn't go with anything else we own. Now's the time to be brutal and admit that it's not something that gets enough wear. The way to make peace with the idea of letting go of these items, particularly the expensive ones, is to think about the person who will make great use out of them.

#3
DO I REALLY NEED THIS?

Continuing with our uncomfortable truths, we quickly hit on the difference between needing and wanting. Some items that made it through the "Do I wear this?" challenge will stumble at this hurdle. Getting into the practice of asking this question of the things you already own will toughen you up for when you're in the changing room of your favourite shop with an armful of sale items!

This question is really useful for recognizing your weaknesses and can help you decide whether you really need six versions of what is more or less the same item. Which grey T-shirt or stripy top do you wear the most often? Is it the highest quality? The one that fits you best? Keep one (or two) and say goodbye to the others.

#4
DOES IT SPARK JOY?

"The question of what you want to own is actually the question of how you want to live your life." Oh, Marie, how do you get it so right? There's a reason why Marie Kondo's style of minimal living hit home with so many of us. This remains a great test for those of us who can rationalize keeping almost anything. The KonMari™ Method advocates getting the whole lot out of your wardrobe and piling it all up on the bed. This can be pretty sobering. The task is then to hold each piece in turn and establish whether it sparks joy. Start with the things you know are fundamental joy-sparkers to get into the rhythm and work your way methodically through the pile. It's okay to have a "maybe" pile. Come back to it at the end.

#5
IS IT SOMETHING I WANT TO TAKE INTO MY FUTURE?

This is a great framing challenge for looking forward and seeing past sentimentality. Many of the items that we needed and wore in the past are not a reflection of where we are going in the future. This question is inspired by the idea of dressing for the job you want, not the job you have. Where do you see yourself in five years' time? Does that person wear these trousers? Even if they suited the old you, does the new you have a different style or needs?

You don't need to be able to predict how fashions will change to take this important step in finding your personal style. This is a time to reflect, give thanks and move on. It's a strange paradox, but taking things away can make it feel like you have a new wardrobe to delve into. It sheds the guilt and gives you a chance to play with the items you know are truly you.

Should it stay or should it go? Questions to ask when having a sort out:

1 Does it still fit?

2 Does it need repair?

3 Does the colour suit you?

4 Does it make you feel good?

5 Does it work with other items you own?

6 Does the fabric feel good against your skin?

7 Has it seen better days?

8 Are you constantly making an adjustment for comfort (e.g. always tugging down a too-short skirt)?

9 When was the last time you wore it?

10 What's stopping you from wearing it this week?

#6
START WITH GREAT UNDERWEAR

Underwear is often an afterthought; many of us still have underwear that was around way before Carrie and Big tied the knot. This often isn't testament to their longevity, but reflects the fact that sorting through our underwear drawer is hardly an appealing task and so often goes to the bottom of our to-do lists. However, confidence in an outfit comes from within, so make sure the first item you put on sets you up for the rest of the day. These items may be unseen, but think of them as a gift to yourself; the foundations on which to proudly build an outfit rather than ashamedly cover up.

Bra-wearing readers, be aware that even the most expensive bras have a lifespan and will stretch out over time. Keep straps well-adjusted and get measured regularly.

What you need from your underwear drawer:

- Most importantly of all: knickers and bras that fit well.

- Items that make you feel confident in any outfit.

- Colours that work with your clothes – have enough black, nude and other colours to suit your needs.

- High-quality socks and tights that won't let you down.

What you don't need:

- Items with holes and worn-out areas. If it can be mended, mend it. If it can't, recycle!

- Ill-fitting underwear that makes you feel self-conscious and physically uncomfortable.

- Garish lingerie that will never see the light of day again.

#7
GET BACK TO BASICS

The concept of a capsule wardrobe is that you have a core set of items that work in multiple ways with many other pieces in your collection. They can all be styled up or styled down to suit the occasion, but they're a great start for getting dressed in the mornings.

FOOLPROOF BASICS THAT DON'T GO OUT OF FASHION INCLUDE THE FOLLOWING:

Plain cotton T-shirt	White shirt	Smart trousers
Jeans	Comfy sweatshirt	Vest top
Well-fitting skirt	Black shift dress	Trainers
Black ankle boots	Ballet pumps	Trench coat

#8
BRING THE ZING WITH INTEREST PIECES

An interest piece is where your personality comes through – the talking point of your outfit. Whether it's the colour, pattern or material, this is the piece under the spotlight. It could be a wrap top that you've made yourself out of a vintage kimono, the perfect organic cotton summer dress with a vibrant print, or a great piece of colourful knitwear. Choose a piece that is unique to you, that you feel great in or that you feel reflects your personality.

Quitting fast fashion shouldn't mean losing the enjoyment of clothes. If anything, it's a chance to really bring to life what you own. It's through interest pieces that you communicate with the world. Some days they'll be more muted, other days they may be attention-grabbing. Either is fine, as long as they reflect you and your mood.

#9
IDENTIFY YOUR COMPLETER PIECES

Layering. It's an art. The third component in the make-up of an outfit is a completer piece. This is the final touch that ties the basics and the interest pieces together. It could be a jacket or a cardigan, shoes, a bag, or simply jewellery or socks. It's that final bit of consideration that can change the way you feel about your entire outfit.

POTENTIAL COMPLETER PIECES INCLUDE THE FOLLOWING ITEMS:

A leather jacket	A blazer	A silk scarf
A cross-body bag	A belt	A gilet (if that's your jam)
A hat	Sunglasses	Unique jewellery

#10
ROTATE

Now you've slimmed down your wardrobe, what next? A fantastic way to make good use of the range of clothes you have is to work from right to left. Once you've washed something, hang it to the left of your wardrobe. The idea is that items which you haven't worn recently find their way to the right of the wardrobe. When you come to pick out an outfit, always start with choosing something from the first few items on the right. You'll soon see if there's something that keeps getting rejected and never seems to fit with the looks you're putting together.

The same principle applies to folded items. If they're stacked, add clean items to the bottom of the pile and pick from the top. If they're KonMari™ed, treat it like a file of library cards, adding to the back and picking from the front. Yes, you can even do this with your underwear!

#11
INVEST IN SEASONAL STORAGE

This is a favourite. It not only makes the most of your space but also gives you the time capsule effect twice a year. As the weather changes, take all of the items that aren't season appropriate out of your wardrobe. The key here is to store your clothes with care so that moths and moisture don't get to them, but they can still breathe.

Firstly, ensure they're clean. This is one of the times when a good airing will not be adequate. Secondly, carefully fold them so they don't form a set of hard-to-remove creases. Some people advocate putting sheets of acid-free tissue paper between each item. A step beyond for some – but the option's there if you choose it! They should then be placed in a breathable zip case, with a little space between your clothes and the top of the case to avoid mustiness. Store them away and look forward to that Christmas-morning feeling when the seasons change.

#12
SORT BY OCCASION

There are items in your wardrobe that you would not wear to a
funeral and items you would not wear to a job interview or a gig.
Keeping the things that are "for best" out of the sequence of rotation
and possibly even out of seasonal storage makes sense, but don't
discount reviewing them every so often as well. Nobody needs stacks
of little black dresses, not matter how easy they are to justify. On a
more practical level, having all of your workwear stored in one place
ready for the week makes compiling outfits that much easier, whether
it's the night before or a mad dash in the mornings.

#13
KNOW WHAT WORKS BEST FOR YOU

We all know that the way that things look on a mannequin is not the way they will look and feel on us, and we don't need the fashion police to point it out to us. However, we may need to fine-tune our sense of which clothes accentuate our assets and which make us focus on our perceived flaws. For example, if you are self-conscious about your long upper body, the likelihood is you'll feel more confident in a high-waisted-something as opposed to low-rise jeans, however on trend they may be. If you have a bigger bust, you may feel freer and more courageous in something that supports you rather than suffering the discomfort of something that squishes you down.

However sentimental you may be about those sinful jeans or boob-crushing jacket, it's better that they go to someone who will wear them and feel great in them rather than letting them take up space and gather dust in a tragic maybe-one-day pile at the back of the wardrobe. Liberate yourself from those maybes.

#14
TRY PROJECT 333™

This is a great challenge. The idea here is to select 33 items that you wear for 3 months, including all accessories, even jewellery and shoes (but excluding underwear). Consider a colour palette before you dive in, as you will then stand a better chance of choosing items that work multiple ways – which really is the aim of the capsule wardrobe game. Similar to the earlier points on basics, interest pieces and completers, think of a set of base colours that can be accentuated with interest colours and prints.

TOP TIP: Ease your way in by selecting 10 items that you will wear for the next 10 days – not dissimilar to holiday packing.

There are many more challenges out there, and taking part in one has several advantages:

- It's proven that you're more likely to achieve a goal if you join a group, and challenges help us to apply this behavioural principle to our wardrobes. Get other like-minded friends on board (see Tip 49 on clothes swaps).

- Beyond your closet, you can challenge your clothes shopping behaviours. No shopping for a certain number of days/weeks/months. You might even achieve a year!

- Challenges posted to Instagram can be fun ways to approach your wardrobe with fresh eyes and get inspiration from others using the hashtag. Usually lasting 30 days with a task each day, these challenges include daily prompts like "Mix at least two textures into your look today" and "Create a look with three levels of layering".

#15
BEAR 30 WEARS IN MIND

Championed by Eco-Age's Livia Firth, this started as a campaign prompting celebrities to be seen on the red carpet in outfits which they had – shock horror – worn before, but quickly evolved into a question that we should all be asking ourselves at the buying stage: Is this something I will wear at least 30 times? This measure can also be used when evaluating the usefulness of the items already in our wardrobes and can be an incentive to wear unloved items more or to pass them onto someone who will get 30 wears out of them.

#16
USE MIRRORS AND DUMMIES

Get a full-length mirror. Not one of the deceptive, concave kinds you can find in changing rooms, just a standard, full-length mirror. You can't truly see how an outfit works unless you can see it all in one go. If you have the space, a tailor's dummy is a great way to try out looks without the sweaty bother of stripping down each time. You can get some beautiful vintage ones if you search for "antique mannequin". Having an outfit hanging on a body makes a big difference to laying it out on a bed. Looking down is not the same as looking at it face on. It's not a vanity thing, it's a reality thing. Which brings us on to the next point...

#17
WHY CHER'S VIRTUAL WARDROBE WASN'T SO CLUELESS

Cher from classic teen movie *Clueless* is not just a style icon for the 1990s but also a role model for great wardrobe management. The source of much teenage envy, Cher's virtual closet enables her to try out different looks on-screen. The reason this paper doll approach works is that knowing how to combine different items in your wardrobe to make a new outfit is a skill. To do this digitally *à la Cher* is a quicker way of trying out multiple looks and looking at them more objectively. The same goes for scrutinizing your look in photographs or video. Many apps now exist to help you catalogue your closet – though apps can't provide you with a perfectly organized rotating wardrobe like Cher's. Sorry!

#18
FOLDING VS HANGING

Knowing how to store your clothes is important. For the same reason that care labels advise you to dry knitwear flat, knits should also be stored folded rather than hung. Over time the sheer weight of the fabric can stretch the shoulders and leave you with a saggy misshapen sack. Shirts and other items that have been meticulously ironed should be hung rather than folded. This will mean less creasing.

Think of the phrase "a place for everything and everything in its place". Knowing where you put your clothes away will ensure you can see and find what you own and therefore make the best use of it.

TOP TIP: Don't you hate those loops that are sewn into the shoulders of some tops and dresses to keep them on their hanger? Just snip them off with the tag when you get your purchase home – they're only there to guard against frantic fingers rifling through clothes on the rail in the shop.

#19
GET A SECOND OPINION

It helps to have a stylish friend on hand with a second opinion.
One of the true friends who's not afraid to be honest with you. This
can help with the "maybe" pile of your sort-through, or to make a
decision on those items that are consistently unworn week after week,
season after season even when you're sure that the right moment just
hasn't presented itself yet.

These beacons of truth can also act as a sounding board for new
combinations you're trying out and may come with their own ideas
and tweaks, such as remembering another piece you hadn't thought
of pairing or adding a French Tuck (tucking a portion of your shirt
in – so named by Tan France of *Queer Eye*). And being the second
opinion can have its own rewards, like getting first dibs on the reject
pile before it makes its way to the thrift shop.

#20
TREASURE WHAT YOU'VE GOT

A big part of enjoying your clothes is the commitment you've made to look after them. In the same way that by joining a gym you're making a promise to your body that you're going to take better care of it, once you've reduced your wardrobe to the quality items, you're going to treat it like an exclusive club where only the best make it past the doorman. In Chapter 5: Making Clothes Last Longer, we go into the ways in which you can extend the active life of your clothing, but this is a moment to make the conscious choice to treasure what you own and stop seeing your clothing as a disposable commodity. Manufacturing methods may have advanced, but each item you own has still passed through multiple pairs of hands to come into existence. Treat yourself, the people in the supply chain and the planet with respect by treasuring what you own.

UPCYCLING
OLD CLOTHES

Now that your closet contains only the treasures that you want to keep, it's time to breathe new life into any old clothes that need a little TLC. According to the not-for-profit group Fashion Revolution, 70% of clothes we throw away have irreversible damage such as colour fading, stubborn stains or shrinking. As frustrating as these casualties can be, they're not a death sentence. By harnessing a little creativity, you can improve on what you had or even transform it into something completely new!

#21
IT DOESN'T HAVE TO BE WACKY

The word "upcycling" brings with it connotations of trashy TV makeover shows that transform homes (not always for the better) on the tightest of budgets. But upcycling can take place without the need of a glue gun. If sequins rock your world, please embellish to your heart's content. If, on the other hand, your style is more understated, you too can use the tips here to make great use of what you already own by extending the lifecycle of your clothes and stamping them with your own style.

#22
MAKE IT ONE OF A KIND

Adjusting your clothing in any way gives you a completely unique piece. Long gone are the days of showing up to the school disco in exactly the same top as your arch nemesis. The clothes you choose to wear are a representation of you; they are a chance to break free of the norm and express yourself to the world. Even small changes will see you build a stronger connection to that item. This is something that sewers, knitters, crocheters and weavers have known since they began their craft. The more time you invest in making an item you love, the stronger the bond you build.

#23
DON'T NEGLECT YOUR SHOES

While on the hunt for your tailor, add a cobbler to your Slow Fashion A-Team. Shoes are a fundamental part of your wardrobe and often take the most wear. Sometimes a pair can be given a new lease of life simply by changing the shoelaces, but for a more substantial overhaul, you'll need a good cobbler.

As with any damage, you're best nipping it in the bud early. As soon as you see signs of wear on a heel or a scuff at the toe, do something about it there and then. Shoe polish may seem archaic, but having a basic set of equipment will come in handy for extending the life of these hard-working items. Polish nourishes the leather, shines it and gives it a layer of defence against wet weather. Trainers shouldn't just be thrown in the wash. There's kit for them, too.

Your shoe care kit may include:

- A large, stiff brush for removing dirt
- Shoe polish in black, brown and neutral
- A shoe brush for each polish and one for wet-cleaning trainers
- A couple of polishing cloths
- A suede brush
- Water-repellent spray
- Microfibre cloth for blotting soapy trainers

#24
GET IT
TAILORED

Tailoring is an amazing skill. We should have no end of admiration
for those skilled artisans able to transform a potato sack into a
perfect-fitting glove for their model. Although many basic alterations
can be done at home or by your local dry cleaner, the more
advanced changes are best left to the experts. The challenge lies in
finding those experts. This is where social enterprise The Seam saw a
gap in the market. They can pair you up with local seamstresses who
are able to do anything from general alterations and repairs through
to made-to-measure evening wear. Tailoring is particularly useful for
vintage pieces that you may have chosen because you love the print,
colour or fabric but the one size available isn't your size. Get it to fit
properly and you'll get endless wear out of it.

#25
ALTER IT

Not all alterations require a trained tailor. Clothes can be transformed by changing a neckline or the length of the sleeves, taking a skirt or dress up or, if there's enough fabric, letting it down, with a few sewing kit basics. Some easy alterations to try:

- Widen a neckline
- Shorten a sleeve
- Re-hem trousers/skirt/dress/shorts to a new length

A bit more advanced:

- Transform a dress into a top and skirt
- Change a collar
- Adjust the fit of a dress or shirt

TOP TIP: Body measurements are most accurately taken by someone else. It's usually easier to take something in than it is to let it out – check the seam widths for extra fabric. Pin into place, measure twice, cut once.

#26
BRING IT UP TO DATE

Instead of buying the latest cut, see if you can adapt something that you already own. Those flared linens are no longer on the Riviera. Time to take them up and in to make yourself a cosmopolitan pair of cropped sailor's trousers that you'll get far more wear out of. Leave enough of a hem to be able to reverse your actions next season.

#27
SWITCH YOUR BUTTONS

If the haberdashers is your sweetshop, there is no finer excuse to dip your hand into the vat of buttons than to make the simplest of changes: new buttons can give your outfit a brand new lease of life. Particularly recommended on coats. Turn something plain into something military, glamorous or even a duffel with the stitch of a button (or toggle).

#28
TRY DYE

Although industrial dyeing is controversial due to the chemicals in the wastewater that it produces, on a smaller scale dyeing can revive clothes that still have plenty of wear in them but have turned that nondescript purple-grey colour through years of washing and sun damage. Giving these items a new lease of life couldn't be easier. Dylon sells single-use dyes in a wide range of colours. which you simply pop in your washing machine.

Dyeing is also a great way of transforming an item which fits well but is missing that special something. Natural dyes using onion skins, turmeric or avocado stones (to name but a few examples) are great to experiment with if you're not wedded to a particular colour result. For the more adventurous, there is always tie-dyeing. Great fun to do but an aesthetic that's not for everyone. For a more fashion-friendly version of the Girl Guide activity, try the different styles of Japanese shibori dyeing, which can give a more geometric result.

#29
BLEACH YOUR WHITES

Used sparingly in a targeted way, bleach shows all other whiter-than-white products who's boss. Let's talk pit stains. Your sweat alone is not the cause of the yellowing. It's the combination of your sweat with bacteria and/or the chemicals in your deodorant. There are natural bleaches that can help – lemon juice or distilled vinegar – but for that white shirt what you really need is bicarbonate of soda and hydrogen peroxide. Mix three parts bicarb to one part water and add a splash of hydrogen peroxide. Scrub into the stain using an old toothbrush and leave it to think about what it's done for at least an hour. Wash in hot water and repeat if necessary.

As with all damage, the earlier you catch it, the better the solution's results. Take the time straight after wear rather than bunging it in the wash and hoping for the best, as this can actually set the stain.

#30
EMBROIDER IT

For stains on colourful items, which may even be caused by bleach, this can be the time to add some embellishment rather than covering them up. Whether it's a leaf, a letter or a simple shape like a triangle, these small additions can be as lavish or as discreet as you like. Not keen on freestyling it? See Tip 99 for our darning instructions, which can be used for covering stains as well as repairing holes. Taking the time to add your own personal touches to an object makes you treasure it all the more for the time that you've put in and for the unique quality you've given it. Now there's not another one like it in the world.

   Use a small embroidery hoop to keep the fabric flat and get stuck into the embroidery floss, using no more than an arm's length at a time (any more may get tangled). Embroidery is a wonderfully therapeutic craft and is as close as most of us will get to living out our Jane Austen fantasies.

#31
THE ART OF SASHIKO

Leading on from embroidery is this traditional Japanese style using cream stitches on indigo fabric. You can create beautiful geometric patterns with a simple running stitch.

Either draw your chosen design onto your fabric using a chalk pencil or a fabric marker or transfer it using dressmaker's carbon paper. You can also buy perforated plastic templates and pre-printed, water-soluble patterns. Once your pattern is in place, thread up and make a small knot at the end of approximately an arm's length of thread. Take your needle for a walk with small, consistently spaced stitches.

This technique can be used for repair, quilting or simply to enhance a feature using its simple but beautiful aesthetic.

#32
BORO IS BEAUTIFUL

The tradition of boro originated in the nineteenth century in the rural north of Japan. Cotton fabric came at a premium and was carefully mended time and time again. Workwear that was damaged beyond repair was used to make family quilts. Each oddly shaped scrap of what was usually indigo-dyed fabric would be laid flat on top of the previous piece and attached using a running stitch (see Tip 31). The effect is a patchwork full of character and layered with history.

These unique items would be passed down through generations, often being embellished to the extent that it was impossible to tell what the original piece had been. Once a source of shame and a mark of poverty, the aesthetic has come full circle and is now honoured by modern Japanese designers.

#33
PATCHWORK YOUR SCRAPS

The more Western style of patchworking has a different history, but still with a level of thriftiness when it came to using mill samples not specifically intended for patchwork. The multi-fabric quilts of Wales and the Pennsylvania Amish display a great deal of skill combined with the practicality of a versatile, functional object. Whether sewn by hand or on a machine, or a combination of the two, patchworking scraps of fabric together into a larger, more usable piece of material is slow but satisfying work. Consider using an appliqué technique to stitch motifs onto existing items of clothing. We go into more detail on patching as a means of repair in Tip 100.

TOP TIP: Consider using patchwork to make a baby blanket out of pre-loved clothes.

#34

ARM WARMERS, MITTS AND GLOVES

A simple yet rewarding project. The most limited level of sewing proficiency and a relatively small amount of fabric is required to create your own cozy fingerless mitts. Accidentally felted cashmere, fleece or any other soft, warm material is perfect for this task – just draw around your hand to create a pattern.

Using the sleeves of a long-sleeved top that you've transformed into a T-shirt works well, too. Hem or overlock the edges and add a few stitches to separate the thumb from the fingers.

#35
UNRAVEL AND RE-MAKE

The cost of yarn is not a meagre one. If there's a cardigan that has sat unworn for seasons on end that you can't bear to part with because of all the love, time and money you poured into it, this may be the time to think about unravelling it and turning the yarn (which you picked for a reason) into something new, something more you. Unravelling is hugely satisfying. Be warned that you may find yourself checking the seams of thrift shop knitwear to see if it's been overlocked or can be unpicked!

You will need:

- A ball winder. Recommended for all knitters, but for a slower wind any tube-like object will do – a roll of cling film is a great alternative.

- A niddy noddy. Definitely not a must-have but satisfying to use. The back of a chair does the same job.

- Some scrap string to tie the skein.

- Weights. Again, be resourceful. If you have an S hook, anything can be a weight.

Unpick or cut the end of the knitting. Wind into a ball or directly round the back of a chair to create a skein. Tie the skein at each end with your scrap yarn to prevent it from tangling. Take it off the chair and admire the crinkles. Wet the whole thing with cool water, give it a squeeze and then hang it up in the shower or over something that will catch the excess water and hook your weight to the bottom of it. Leave to dry completely, then wind into a ball ready to be re-knit.

TOP TIP: Always unravel from the bound-off edge. These were the last stitches to be knit, and starting here will make life infinitely easier than attempting to unravel from the cast-on edge.

#36
BAGS AND CASES

Almost any fabric can be turned into a bag or case of some description. Here are a few ideas to get you going:

- SHOPPING BAG: Make your own reusable tote. Cut the handles from the same piece of material if possible. A no-sew T-shirt upcycle option simply involves cutting fringing along the bottom and knotting the front to the back to create the bottom of the bag. Then chop the sleeves off and use the arm holes as your handles.

- PRODUCE BAGS: Use a lightweight fabric to make your own produce bags. Sew two squares of your desired size around three edges. Keeping the bag inside out, roll the top over about 2.5cm (1in) and sew around the circumference, leaving enough space for your drawstring cord to fit through. Snip the stitches in the seams of this small section and use a safety pin to shuffle your drawstring through, then knot the ends of your drawstring together.

- GLASSES CASE: The same principle as the produce bags but made as a narrow rectangle to fit your glasses. Use a synthetic material to prevent scratching your lenses while they're stored.

- LAPTOP/TABLET CASES: Create a denim, felt or quilted envelope to safely store your tech. Add an elasticated band to tuck the top flap into, or a popper, button or Velcro closure.

#37
SCRUNCHIES

A satisfying and quick project that makes a great gift.
  You will need:

- A rectangle of fabric approximately 30cm x 12cm (12in x 5in)

- Some elastic

Method:

1   Fold your fabric lengthways with right sides facing.

2   Sew all the way along the edge to make a long tube.

3   Turn your tube right side out.

4   Thread your elastic through.

5   Knot your elastic to create a loop of approximately 15cm (6in).

6   Tuck the raw edges in and hand-sew the ends together using an invisible stitch to complete the loop. Voilà!

#38
FOR THE HOME

Some items are beyond repair. A sad example of this is if a knit has been felted in the wash. There's no going back and it's of no use to friends or the thrift shop. Don't despair – there's still use in it yet. Only the most basic of sewing skills are required to turn a piece of fabric into a cushion cover, using any pre-existing buttons and buttonholes on the garment as the closing mechanism. The best upcycled cushion covers come from cabled knitwear. You can even stuff your cushion with scrap fabric.

Rag rugs are another classic homeware upcycle hack. You can either hook strips of fabric through a mesh canvas or sacking or go all out with a woven rug which, FYI, the likes of Anthropologie sell at an eye-watering price.

One more way to give a new life to a damaged garment is by cutting it up into cleaning cloths. Suitable for many household chores, these are a no-brainer.

#39
FOR THE PETS

Let's not forget our fur babies. Old clothes can be repurposed into bedding, supervised tug toys, catnip cushions or dog or horse coats. You've not lived until you've seen a sock transformed into a rat gilet. Fabulous! Challenge yourself and your sewing skills — worth it for your pet's sheer look of disgust if nothing more.

#40
FOR THE KIDS

The cutest upcycle for kids has to be the transformation of unwanted items into an animal costume. But besides fancy dress, your wardrobe rejects provide more than enough fabric to make your mini-you at least a smaller version of the original. Matching parent–child outfits are optional. Take it one step further into the world of miniature by making toys' clothes.

Upping the ante on the simple sock puppet, the most kid-friendly upcycle award goes to the sock monkey. To make your very own, you will need:

- A pair of socks. Odd socks are fine.

- Needle and thread.

- Stuffing or scrap material to use as stuffing.

- Felt, buttons or googly eyes depending on the age of the recipient.

1   Turn your socks inside out.

2   Place Sock 1 front-down on the table, with the toe at the top, heel facing you. Cut through both layers of sock from the middle of the cuff to the heel. These are Monkey's legs. The heel is Monkey's bum.

3   Sew all around the open edges of the legs, leaving a small gap so you can turn Monkey right side out and stuff his/her torso and legs.

4   Once Monkey is stuffed, sew up the small gap.

5   Take Sock 2. Cut the heel off to use as Monkey's muzzle.

6   The arms are made using the same part of the sock as you used to make the legs, so cut through both layers of Sock 2 from the cuff to the heel. When you reach the heel, cut them off.

7   Sew the length and across one of the short ends of each of Monkey's arms. Turn them inside out and stuff. Attach to torso.

8   Sew Sock 2's heel to the middle of Monkey's face for the muzzle, leaving a small gap. Stuff and then sew shut.

9   Use some of the remainder of Sock 2 to make your Monkey a tail and ears (stuffing optional) and stitch or glue on the eyes.

10 Bonus points for eccentric monkey coiffure and cute ensemble.

STAYING
ON TREND

From borrowing and lending to making your own clothes, explore ways you can update what you own or get something "new" without the need for the quick fix of fast fashion. Let's start with being clear on trends vs fashion and getting the most out of what you already own through the ways you wear and style your clothes.

#41
STYLISH ≠ TRENDY

A trend is a fad. It comes and, before long, it goes. Some trends will resonate with you and some won't, but the most stylish people don't bend to every trend. They stay true to what they know their style to be. What makes people stylish is not their status, age or body shape, but rather the way that they wear their clothes.

There will be people whose style you admire, but simply replicating their wardrobe won't emulate their look. Zoom in a little closer and work out what it is about the fit of what they're wearing, the extra touches, the partly rolled sleeve, the mix of colour or pattern choices, the way they hold themselves. You may really be drawn to the confidence that they exude.

#42
IDENTIFY YOUR SIGNATURE STYLE

Style confidence comes not from reinventing yourself every season according to the trends but from staying true to yourself: knowing what suits you and being the trend you want to see. Your wardrobe sort-through should have given you a sense of the looks you return to year on year. Think of the pieces that you get complimented on; the chances are that they fit you really well. Ask for a second opinion: What does your best friend consider to be "you"?

As important as identifying what you like is knowing what you dislike. It could be a colour that washes you out or a material that you hate the feel of; you may have pushed on with an item because it was on trend but the fit wasn't right. These things are good to be aware of so that you can quickly bypass them if they come around again.

#43
MAKE A
MOOD BOARD

A mood board is a great way to inspire you and to have a quick visual reference of the looks that you're drawn to. It can be interesting to see how this evolves over time and what common themes crop up season after season. Pinterest can be a really useful tool for storing these looks. Their algorithm then serves you up similar looks and styles. It's also a retro pleasure to crack out the glue stick, compiling images from magazines into a scrapbook.

#44
FIND NEW STYLE INSPIRATION

Your style icons don't have to come from the world of celebrity, or even this century. What are the eras you love? They don't need to be copied to the note but they will give you a sense of the shapes you like. Who are the real-life people you know whose style you admire? Chances are it's their consistency, confidence and eye for great design that you admire, not their ability to buy a whole new wardrobe every season. Influencers are called influencers for a reason. Brands invest in these people to promote their products because of their following and their ability to create engaging content. By all means appreciate their aesthetic, but be mindful that they are able to wear a new outfit in each photo because a lot of it is gifted to them.

#45
UNSUBSCRIBE AND UNFOLLOW

The power of marketing should not be underestimated; take steps to stop the barrage of sales messages. They seem innocent enough until you realize you've been browsing a brand's website for almost an hour with a cart full of "maybes", returning to old habits where you justify a made-up need triggered by the price. Scroll down to the bottom of each marketing email and click "unsubscribe". It will ask you: "Are you sure?" Yes, you're sure.

The same goes for social accounts that serve to ensnare rather than inspire you. A quick, painless unfollow will soon see less temptation weaselling its way into your everyday activities. It may sound cynical, but if marketing didn't work, companies wouldn't invest millions in it. Outsmart the Mad Men by consciously closing the door on them.

#46
FOCUS ON ACCESSORIES

Instead of feeling the need to buy a whole new outfit, why not scale it down to one well-made accessory that encapsulates the style of that season? A statement necklace, earrings or even a new make-up look can be enough to transform the items you already own and are fun to experiment with! The key here is to advance and enhance your style rather than a complete overhaul. Whether your personality is more classic or more glamorous, you can reflect this through your accessories.

Other accessories to consider:

- Shoes
- Handbags
- Bracelets
- Rings
- Hair accessories
- Belts
- Hats
- Scarves

#47
ONE IN, ONE OUT

Maintain the ruthless mindset you got into when reassessing your wardrobe in Chapter 1; now's not the time to find fast fashion workarounds to fill it back up again. Be strict with yourself. You know you can get by with fewer, great quality pieces. If a new jacket has made the cut, is there another jacket that you can say goodbye to? Don't let that capsule expand to the size where it's hard to swallow.

#48
IT'S NOT ABOUT LABELS

Great design is great design. It's not because it's from a particular brand or fashion house that it's a sure-fire winner. Being top to toe in designer labels gives off a message, but that message is not necessarily one of style. Cast your mind back a few years, and remember that mixing designer with high street was a trend of its own. Though not shouted about in the same way, it remains this curation of pieces from different sources that makes for an interesting and individual style, not being a walking billboard for any one shop or designer.

#49
CLOTHES
SWAPS

Clothes swaps are a great, sociable, cost-efficient way to refresh the contents of your wardrobe. Whether among friends or at an organized event, the idea is that no money changes hands, but you leave with no more than the number of items that you brought with you in the first place (keeping to the one in, one out principle). Pro events often also include fashion brands' over-produced pieces.

There is nothing like that altruistic feeling of someone picking up and getting excited about an item that's been lying dormant at the back of your cupboard. As ever, try not to get swept up in the moment too much and take only things that you really need and will wear.

#50
THRIFT SHOPS

It will come as no surprise to many of you that thrift shops are brimming with gems. Many people advocate checking out the thrift shops in more affluent areas for the most precious cast-offs. Although there is some reason to this logic, the people who work in such areas tend to know the value of what they're putting on the hangers and price accordingly. It's not always the items donated directly to that store that are sold there, so do shop around.

Unsurprisingly, in recent years there has been a rise in poor quality, fast fashion items making their way onto the rails of thrift shops. These are the clothes that many people find it easiest to say goodbye to, perpetuating the cycle of disposable, cheap clothing. However, a light rummage should dig out the goodies.

Top things to be on the lookout for are as follows:

- QUALITY FABRIC: Check the care label to see its composition. A high percentage of natural fibres such as cotton, wool, silk or linen are what to look for. With time, you'll get to know fabrics by touch. It's always interesting to check the care label to confirm your suspicions, or surprise you by how deceptive polyester can be.

- SEAM ALLOWANCE: Having a little more fabric hidden in the seam will enable you to let an item out or use a matching swatch for patching if it gets damaged in the future. It's usually a sign of quality and longevity and something to get nerdily excited about.

- HANDMADE ITEMS: Whether knitted or sewn, these are easy to spot by the lack of overlocked stitches and care labels. Hand-knitted items are the easiest to unravel and hand-sewn items tend to be made of great quality material, finished off with up to a couple of inches of extra fabric in the seams.

- GO BEYOND BASICS: Of the basics, interest and completer pieces mentioned in Chapter 1, thrift shops are best for interest and completer pieces to add a flourish to your well-fitting basics.

- THE CHANGING ROOM: It may look fantastic on the hanger and have your size written on its label but it can look completely different on. Please don't skip this step. Look out for more detail on the importance of trying things on in Chapter 4.

#51
VINTAGE

Vintage ticks so many boxes. You'll find something unique, often at a great price, and the quality can be fantastic. There are lots of sellers out there with a brilliant eye for curating exquisite finds. Look for some that match your style and build your relationship with them so you come to mind when they're on the hunt themselves.

Shops and markets are great if you're up for a rummage, but admiring from afar on Instagram or digital channels can save you from the feeling of not wanting to walk away empty-handed, which can lead to impulse purchases. By all means use vintage as your interest pieces but be mindful of the questions in Chapter 1 and make sure you're going to get upwards of 30 wears out of it.

#52
EBAY

It giveth and it taketh away. eBay is a great place to bargain hunt and perfect for those who enjoy the thrill of the chase. It's also the first place to go to list your pre-loved items.

Buying:

- Search for spelling mistakes. You'll be amazed by the items that have been missed because the person listing them misspelled "Versace".

- As with any auction, decide on a figure you're willing to part with and stick to it – it can be easy to get swept up in the excitement of the last 30 seconds, but this way expensive lies.

Selling:

- PHOTOGRAPHY IS KEY. Hang it up, light it well. The more photos, the better. If you want to show how it looks on a person, use a tailor's dummy – it can be off-putting to buyers to see it on an actual person, even with the head cropped out.

- RELEASE YOUR INNER COPYWRITER. This is your chance to sell, sell, sell! Get descriptive, suggest ways in which it can be worn, give your reason for parting with it. The clearer you can be, the less time you'll spend answering the same questions over and over. You can always update the listing with more information once it's gone live.

- OVERSTATE ANY DAMAGE. It's better to give too much information and for buyers to be pleasantly surprised than to hope it will go unnoticed. Photograph any snags, stains or holes and describe the cause and possibly a solution in the description.

#53
DEPOP

----

eBay's younger, more fashionable sibling, Depop is mostly fashion and beauty and has a younger audience. App-based, it describes itself as "The creative community's mobile marketplace". It's not an auction in the same way as eBay. When selling, state your price and be prepared for messages asking if the item is still available and attempts to wrangle a cheeky deal. The same goes the other way: it's perfectly acceptable to get in touch and ask the seller if they would be willing to take a lower amount. You might get a "no", but other sellers enjoy a bit of bartering and if you don't ask, you don't get.

TOP TIP: Unlike with eBay, it is more acceptable here to show pictures of you wearing what you're selling. Get creative with backgrounds and hashtags.

#54
HAND-ME-DOWNS

Gone is the shame associated with an older sibling's hand-me-down. Instead, see it as a chance to swoop in on the investments of a relative or friend before they make it to the thrift shop. If you're of a similar size and love each other's style, why not organize a swap between the two of you? If they're about to list their items on eBay, save them the hassle (and the commission) by offering them some cash to take it off their hands.

It's hugely satisfying to see the excitement and gratitude of the person who is going to take an unwanted (by you) piece of clothing into the next chapter of its adventure. Warning: Seeing an item you parted with looking fabulous styled differently on someone else can bring out your inner frenemy!

#55
BORROW AND LEND

Got "nothing to wear" for a costume party or a one-off event? Try putting some feelers out among your friends to see if they have something they can lend you for the day. It doesn't have to be an entire outfit; just one interest piece (see Chapter 1) can transform the things which you already own and make you feel that you have a whole new look. Carefully launder and return in good time, possibly with a bar of chocolate! What goes around comes around, so be sure to return the favour when you can.

You can also lend what you have outside of your friendship circle using apps like By Rotation. List your items with the dates that they're available and a price, and await rental requests.

#56
RENT

As part of Generation Rent, renting instead of owning applies to everything from homes and cars to music and films. Why not then rent your clothes? There is no shortage of recent businesses that have sprung up offering their service to facilitate just that. Examples are Bundlee or Upchoose for baby clothes and Girl Meets Dress or Rent the Runway for womenswear. To date, there aren't many menswear equivalents and the cynics say that this is because men tend to be less fickle with fashion.

#57
SHOP FABRICS, NOT CLOTHES

How do you guarantee that the clothes you wear are made of the finest quality fabrics? Walk past the clothes shops and straight to the fabric shop! By taking your clothing journey back a step, you won't need to compromise on fit or colour. Instead of replacing one vice with another, this tends to be a more expensive and therefore generally more thought-out purchase. Give the fabric a scrunch and a stretch to get a sense of how it will crease and give.

   It's best to go with an item of clothing in mind, or better still, a sewing pattern, to ensure you come away with enough of a suitable material. Similarly, buying too much fabric is not only costly but generally leaves you without quite enough to make another garment. A pattern will give you clear guidance on quantities for each size and give adjustments based on the different widths of fabric rolls available.

TOP TIP: Beginners are best off starting with a non-stretch cotton with a clear "right" and "wrong" side. Hold off on the stretch, sheer, lace, crepes and metallics until you're a few garments down.

#58
LEARN HOW TO READ A SEWING PATTERN

Once you've cracked the jargon, you'll have unlocked a world of possibility. There are so many fantastic modern patterns out there. Check out Tilly and the Buttons and Merchant & Mills to start.

- SELVEDGE: The selvedge is the self-finished edges of the roll of fabric, i.e. not the part that has been cut.

- GRAINLINE: A large double-headed arrow on each pattern piece shows you the direction in which the piece should be laid (the grainline) – parallel to the selvedge.

- SEAM ALLOWANCE: Most patterns incorporate a seam allowance, often around 1.5cm ($^5/_8$in). This lets you know how far you need to sew from the edge.

- NOTCHES AND TAILOR'S TACKS: These marks are included on pattern pieces so that you can line separate pieces up when you sew your garment together. Notches are V shapes and tailor's tacks are circles. Both can be marked onto your fabric using a variety of methods, including tailor's chalk or washable fabric pen.

TOP TIP: Wash your fabric before cutting any pattern pieces, as most fabrics shrink a little during their first wash.

#59
DUST OFF THE SEWING MACHINE

Most of the projects in Chapter 2 can be done by hand, but for making clothes you'll want to get hold of a sewing machine. It's not a huge investment, you may even already have one in the family, and it will last you a lifetime. Here's a whistle-stop tour of the basics:

- THREADING YOUR MACHINE: Each stitch is formed from two threads: one from the top spool that sits on top of your machine, one from the bobbin that sits under your needle plate. Most newer models of sewing machines have numbers that take you through the steps of threading your machine. Follow the instruction booklet until it comes as second nature. Make sure your bobbin is wound with a healthy amount of the same colour thread as your spool.

- TENSION: This ensures you have an even stitch that takes equal amounts of thread from the top and the bottom. Test your tension on a scrap of doubled fabric before you start. If the bottom thread can be seen on the top of your fabric or the fabric is puckering, your tension is too tight. If there are loops forming on the underside of the fabric your tension is too loose. Adjust accordingly.

- SEWING STRAIGHT AND EVEN: Take it slow and let the machine work. You shouldn't be pulling or pushing your fabric through the machine; simply guide it. There are markings on the needle plate to show you the distance from your needle to the edge of your fabric (the width of the seam allowance), but you can also use a piece of masking tape to mark the edge if your seam is wider than the plate.

TOP TIP: Make a toile, or muslin. This is a test run of a garment using calico, which is much cheaper to make mistakes with. It will familiarize you with the pattern and the fit ahead of going for gold on the real deal.

#60
LEARN TO KNIT OR CROCHET

Transforming a single strand into a wearable item is as rewarding as the process itself. If you have never knitted before or need a refresher, pick up a set of 4mm (size 8 UK, 6 US) needles, a skein of DK yarn in a colour that you like and follow some YouTube tutorials until you get the hang of it. Alternatively, get hold of a kit. Wool and the Gang and Stitch & Story mark their kits with the level of experience needed. Embrace any imperfections and enjoy the satisfaction that comes from being able to say, "I made that!"

SHOPPING
MORE
EFFICIENTLY

The stark realities that we touch on in this chapter are here to arm you with the tools you need to make more conscious decisions rather than to put you off fashion altogether. Loving fashion shouldn't have to come at a cost to our planet or to the people behind the scenes, and this chapter shows you what you can do to make a difference. If you have ever had any doubts about your decision to quit fast fashion, it's time to leave them behind.

#61
BE CONSCIOUS ABOUT YOUR CONSUMPTION

There is a lot of debate around whether the responsibility for the fast fashion crisis lies on the shoulders of shoppers, the fashion industry or the government, and the fact is that it spreads across all three. The uncomfortable truth is that if the demand from customers disappeared, businesses would have to change their ways of working to remain viable. This book advocates shopping less but also looks to arm you with the information you need to make informed decisions when you do shop. The way to combat fast fashion lies in putting control back in the hands of the customer and for us all to vote with our wallets: shopping the change we want to see.

#62
SHOP LESS

The simplest and often the most difficult principle when it comes to breaking up with fast fashion is to shop less. Dame Vivienne Westwood herself states: "Buy less, choose well, make it last", and this has become the mantra of slow fashion. Shopping better means shopping less, in terms of both frequency and quantity. Rather than seeing clothes shopping as a social activity or as a hobby, it's time to look at it in a similar light as shopping for food and other necessities. This may seem like the most killjoy part of the process, but by being abstemious, you will have a heightened enjoyment (and more money to spend) when you do go on the hunt for a specific item – and as Chapter 3 showed, you'll be no less fashionable for it.

#63
SHOP ALONE

Buzz-kill strikes again: it's well-known that shopping on your own makes you more likely to stick to your guns and not succumb to purchasing something you don't need. Many of us have been that friend who gets caught up in the moment, encouraging someone we're shopping with to "just get it!" or, in the name of good friendship, assuring them it looks amazing and that they can't live without it. There's no end to our creativity when it comes to justifying the decision to buy, and having a trusty sidekick who wants to give us a confidence boost makes the temptation all the more potent. By all means, get a second opinion – but that's what the changing room selfie is for.

#64
SHOP IRL (WHEN YOU CAN)

Shopping for clothes should be a sensory experience. Feeling the fabric's softness, weight and strength. Seeing the colours in different lights. Seeing how the piece hangs on you. With fast fashion brands offering free returns, the temptation to shop online is huge; buying items in multiple sizes, or buying several options in the hunt for one outfit. It can be an easy, quick pick-me-up when you're feeling slobby and a glamorous transformation is only a click away.

But the fashion industry already has a massive carbon footprint and this sending back and forth only adds to it. Brands are banking on us keeping both options, often because we're too busy to make the returns or miss the window. And if you do return it? Those items are often not resold but destroyed, as it's more cost-efficient. Getting it right the first time is much more likely when safely shopping in person.

#65
KNOW
YOUR SIZE

Unlike men's trousers, which tend to come sized by waist measurement, women face the challenge of a different approach to sizing in each shop, and shopping for vintage by the size on the label can be even more challenging. A UK size 12 in 1970 had a waist measurement of just under 24 inches (60 cm), while in 2011 the same size had a waist of just under 30 inches (76 cm). Without standardization, manufacturers were left to define sizes as they saw appropriate. And so, they took it upon themselves to implement so-called "vanity sizing". Fashion houses try to design for the average person, but as we all know, the average person simply doesn't exist. No clothing size chart knows you better than you know yourself, so don't take labels at their word and make sure you…

#66
TRY IT ON

When there's a huge queue for the changing rooms and you can't face the faff of stripping down, it can be tempting to buy an item to try on at home (with the full intention of returning it if it's not right). We all know how that ends.

Slow fashion means slow shopping. How it looks on the hanger is not the same as how it looks and feels on. As we know, the sizing varies from shop to shop and there are a few fitting details that you won't know until you've worn it:

- Does it fit you on the shoulders?

- Are the sleeves the right length?

- Does it pull around the bust?

- Does it come up too short or too long?

- Is there room to fit two fingers between your body and the waistband?

- Are the pockets gaping?

- Can you comfortably sit down?

- Does it ride up when you walk?

TOP TIP: Don't compromise on any of the above. Odd fits are particularly prominent on the sale rail – there's often a reason why those particular items are discounted.

#67
UNDERSTAND YOUR WEAKNESSES

Whether it's practicality – "this will be so useful" – or a colour that you're always drawn to, or simply a thing for spots/stripes/gingham (delete as appropriate), you can have enough of a good thing. Knowing your wardrobe kryptonite will keep you mindful in your selection process. That's not to say you should steer away from the things you like – far from it – and as we saw in Chapter 1, it's important to know what your style is. But now that you are very familiar with the contents of your pared-down wardrobe, knowing what your weaknesses are puts you in a stronger position when coming face to face with variations of something you already own.

#68
BUY CHEAP, BUY TWICE

The convenience of disposable, single-use items is a relatively new concept. Our throwaway society only really emerged in the 1950s as as mass production led to time-saving solutions, not just in fashion but across the board. It's only now that we are seeing the devastating effects of substituting quality for convenience. We buy cheap, we don't take care of what we have and when this cheaply made item falls apart, we throw it in the bin and get another one. The problem with buying things that aren't made to last is that although we may not directly see the impact, someone, somewhere is paying the true cost of our actions. The 30 Wears challenge in Tip 15 taught us that we're better off spending a reasonable amount on something that's made to last than buying something for half the price that wasn't made to survive more than a few months of wear. Companies such as BuyMeOnce have curated brands with this ethos so that you can shop anything from socks to kitchen utensils that will last. If it's not worth mending, it's not worth buying in the first place.

#69
BEWARE THE BARGAIN

A dress for less than the price of a cup of coffee democratizes fashion – everyone loves a bargain, right? The old saying about being too good to be true certainly applies in the case of low-priced clothes. The reason a dress can be sold at that price is because of exploitation of many of the most vulnerable communities of the world. Slave and child labour are commonplace in the fashion industry supply chain, as are unsafe working conditions. With over half of the price of a garment going on brand and retail mark-ups, what percentage of that dress do you think the person that made it will receive? Pennies, if anything.

In fact, shockingly, the garment worker receives only 0.6% of the average breakdown of the cost of a T-shirt, according to the Clean Clothes Campaign:

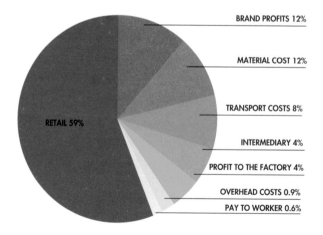

BRAND PROFITS 12%

MATERIAL COST 12%

TRANSPORT COSTS 8%

INTERMEDIARY 4%

PROFIT TO THE FACTORY 4%

OVERHEAD COSTS 0.9%

PAY TO WORKER 0.6%

RETAIL 59%

#70
KNOW THE ORIGIN

The fashion supply chain is a complex one. With the amount of
subcontracting that takes place, it can be almost impossible, even
for the brands themselves, to truly know the origin of an item of
clothing. A good place to start is to check the country on the label.
There are many manufacturers across the globe upholding great
working practices. However, be aware that it's possible to mark
something as made in the UK even if the only work that took place
in the UK was adding the finishing touches. Most fast fashion is
made in China and Bangladesh, where it becomes more difficult
to trace an item back to its source and where the laws are more
lenient regarding working hours and conditions than they are in
the EU, for example. It's not as clear-cut as simply not buying from
these countries – there are many manufacturers across the globe
upholding great working practices – but if your aim is to get back
to the source, it's a difficult road to follow unless you buy from a
brand with a transparent supply chain.

#71
WHO MADE YOUR CLOTHES?

A fantastic campaign launched by Fashion Revolution's Orsola de Castro and Carry Somers unveils the faces behind your clothes. It's a stark but effective reminder that each seam of every garment you own has been sewn by someone. It can be all too easy to forget that each item will have passed through an average of 60 pairs of hands before it reaches yours. Seeing into the eyes of the person, so often anonymous, who made your clothes leads to a human connection that goes deeper than any label ever could. Thinking about the actual people behind the clothes and the skill and time that has gone into cutting, sewing and finishing your item is guaranteed to give you pause next time you consider buying a quick-fix outfit.

#72
WHAT'S IT MADE OF?

One component of Fashion Revolution's global campaign asks, "What's in my clothes?" There are pros and cons to each type of fibre. As with many slow fashion decisions, there's not one simple answer. While we might instinctively opt for natural fibres such as cotton, wool and linen, there is no wonder fabric that ticks all the boxes. We need to consider the impact of the processes on the environment as well as the workers, from extracting the raw material all the way through to the end of the garment's life.

FIBRE	PRO	CON
Cotton	Soft and breathable	The thirstiest of plants. Studies have shown that growing cotton for one pair of jeans uses the equivalent of between five and ten years' of drinking water for one person.
Wool	Warm and durable	Sheep emit methane (to put it politely). Animal welfare is not always traceable and therefore wool is shunned by many vegans. Can be itchy.
Linen	Lightweight and twice as strong as cotton	Creasing and poor elasticity mean it's not as versatile as other fibres. Processing can release chemicals into waterways.
Silk	Luxurious feel and natural sheen; hypoallergenic	The fabric is expensive and difficult to care for. Silkworms are killed during production, unless you use "peace silk".
Bamboo	Soft, strong and regenerates quickly	Extracting the fibre often involves a chemically intensive process.
Synthetics (Polyester, nylon and acrylic)	Cost-efficient, durable and blend well with other fibres	Man-made from petrochemicals, these fibres do not biodegrade. They release plastic microfibres with every wash. Sweaty to wear.

#73
THINK ABOUT THE END OF ITS LIFE

Are you familiar with planned obsolescence? It's personified by the tech giants. You used to be able to take your computer apart to add more RAM and replace the battery. Now it's all glued into place so that instead of replacing components when needed, you have to buy a whole new computer. The circular economy is the antithesis of this. It promotes not only making things last longer but also being able to return the item to its original materials at the end of its life, ready to be used again. This puts the onus on businesses to consider the lifecycle of the product, right from the design phase.

When selecting fibres, think about the synthetic components that will not biodegrade. Can they be recycled? Once the item no longer serves a purpose for you, where will it go? Having a more sustainable wardrobe means doing what we can as consumers to keep our clothing for longer and avoid having it end up in landfill or incinerated.

#74
THINK ABOUT THE PLANET

Many of the processes of industry have a negative impact on the planet. From the pesticides used in the growing phase, to the contaminated waste water being pumped back into local water sources in the dyeing stage, through to the carbon produced by transporting these goods around the world. By getting a deeper understanding of the origin of the items we buy (see Tip 70), we can make choices to be a more conscious consumer. Wherever you are in the world, which fibres are produced in your country? Do they have an organic variant? What dyes do they use? Wool, for example, comes in many different natural shades; can we embrace these in order to bypass the often-thirsty process of dyeing altogether?

#75
SHOP LOCAL

One of the easiest ways to support your local area is to shop from local businesses. A lot of the money spent locally will be reinvested locally, as these businesses buy from other businesses nearby. These shops also give the individual character to an area; they are the community as opposed to being in the community as a larger brand might be.

Shopping locally and in person enables you to make wiser decisions, both for the reasons listed at the beginning of this chapter and because you can ask questions of the knowledgeable people who work in your local shops, building all-important human relationships along the way. If the items on sale are also produced locally, it means that you are supporting employment in the area and that the carbon impact is lower. It feels like a small change, but it has a major trickle-down effect.

#76
SHOP INDEPENDENT

There's a quote that says when you shop from a small business, an actual person does a little happy dance. It's true! Small businesses make up an important part of the economy. By choosing to shop independent, your money isn't evaporating into big business. Supporting artisans means investing in an entrepreneur who took a chance. You get a more personal service and a higher level of care because these small businesses are an extension of the founders themselves. You're likely to see more originality and innovation from these smaller enterprises who are more adept at trying out new ideas and have the incentive to really focus on the detail. Ultimately, you're helping real people do what they do better.

#77
BEWARE OF GREENWASHING

Greenwashing is the phenomenon where, without changing their previous practices, brands have seen the consumer desire for more sustainable items and tried to align their brand with that behaviour. It's the fashion equivalent of rubbing a bit of soil on your genetically modified veg and calling it organic. But by simply questioning what is presented to us, we can see these businesses for what they really are. Watch out for the following greenwashing giveaways:

1   Unsubstantiated language. "Eco this" and "zero waste that" mean nothing if they can't supply any further detail.

2   The power of imagery. Using colours, icons and images associated with freshness and growth has been used to cover up a more polluting reality.

3   Green marketing talking the talk when key elements of the business are not walking the walk. This can be seen in factions of certain fast fashion brands that promote themselves as "conscious".

4   Facts without back-up. Can claims be substantiated? Does the endorsement come from a real person?

5   It looks too good to be true. Scratch the surface; the reality is that it most likely is.

#78
SEEK TRANSPARENCY

It is a minefield, but there are certifications in place to give accreditation to brands who have considered and conscientiously investigated each stage of their business, including B-Corp Certification and the Global Organic Textile Standard (GOTS). Indeed, many brands out there pride themselves on their sustainable ethics and credentials, but it's still good to approach them with a healthy scepticism. Look for transparency; they should be able to answer the following questions:

People – who made my clothes?

- Are they of legal working age?
- Are they safe?
- Are they paid the minimum or living wage?
- Have you visited the factory?
- What made you choose that manufacturer?

Planet – how has it been made?

- Where was the garment made?
- What is the garment made of?
- Where was the material sourced from?
- What are the finishing techniques involved?
- Can I buy the equivalent made locally?

#79
'TIS ALWAYS THE SEASON

Fashion collections used to be released twice a year: Spring/Summer and Autumn/Winter. However, to keep up with consumer demand, the high street now releases up to 20 collections per year, even more for the online fast fashion giants. Overproduction is an issue, no matter where the brand sits on the luxury scale, and destroying unsold merchandise is common practice, preventing it from being sold at too low a price and potentially "damaging the brand". This burning or shredding is grossly unethical.

To counter seasonality some brands are creating seasonless collections. This has the advantage of giving clothes a timelessness while also reaching a wider audience with differing climates. Look at ways in which clothes can be layered to work all year round, making sure that your outfit is for more than just one season.

#80

BE CONSISTENT; BE PICKY

You have the know-how, you have the reasons why. Now stick to your guns. Old habits die hard, but you're not alone in this journey – and it is a journey. If you question each purchase and scrutinize your decisions, you will be shopping better. Buying less fast fashion is a good start, but going cold turkey on it altogether is doable and hugely beneficial, to you and the planet. Better than any slogan T-shirt, you'll be wearing the change you want to see in the world.

MAKING CLOTHES LAST LONGER

The relationship we have with our clothes should be built on mutual trust. Your clothes work hard for you and in return you take care of them to the best of your ability. We know from Fashion Revolution that extending the life of clothing by just a further nine months would reduce carbon, waste and water footprints by around 20–30% each. To extend that life we need to wash each item more effectively and know what to do to prevent and repair any damage that occurs.

So, in this final chapter, we're going to have a good wash, then we'll go into identifying damage and repair methods you can use to get more life out of the clothes you love.

#81
UNDERSTAND CARE LABELS AND GET TO KNOW YOUR MACHINE

A string of symbols can usually be found on a label inside our garments, but what do all the symbols mean? They are genuinely there to help us, but it can feel like learning another language. Getting this right is the most important part of making your clothes last longer, since irreversible damage like colour fading and shrinking come about when we don't care for items properly. Knowing your care symbols opens up the options of your washing machine's functionality so that you're no longer going for the default 40°C (105°F) cotton wash but instead you're customizing each cycle to your clothes' needs. From the triangle of bleach, to the circle of dry clean, a quick online search can provide you with your complete care label guide. Top tip: Keep a copy by your washing machine.

#82
WASH LESS, AIR MORE

This is the point where a lot of people turn their noses up, but we don't actually need to wash every item between wears. We're not talking about your gym kit and undies here, but clothes that have had only light wear don't need to be washed so frequently. We'll cover the benefits of sunlight at a later point, but even popping something on a hanger outside your wardrobe overnight should give it enough of an airing to be good to go for another day. You can give it a spritz with an odour-eliminating product if that makes you feel more confident. You can even make your own with a little bicarb, fabric softener and warm filtered water. Go on, give it another wear!

#83
SPOT-CLEAN STAINS

Slopped down yourself? It happens to the best of us. The temptation is to fling it straight in the wash or onto the laundry pile where the stain will really have a chance to sink in. Stop right there! Use a damp cloth and a touch of detergent to rub the stain, rinse and leave to air dry. Pre-treat any major stains before putting a wash on – try the following home remedies for the most stubborn marks.

Salt and washing up liquid
Apply salt to soak up any excess liquid followed by washing up liquid or liquid detergent
*   Grease, fat and red wine

White vinegar
Either soak or dab to saturate the area.
*   Best for coffee and blood

Rubbing alcohol or hand sanitizer
Mix equal parts hand sanitizer and water. Spray onto the back of the stain and blot with kitchen towel.
*   Grass, ink and lipstick

Milk or cream
Chocolate needs more dairy! Milk or cream will help dilute the stain before it goes into the wash.
*   Chocolate

#84
TURN IT INSIDE OUT AND USE A LAUNDRY BAG

This is especially important for T-shirts with motifs and colourful prints: turning your clothes inside out means they come up against less friction. To protect delicate clothes, make sure you use laundry bags – which are also handy for small items like sports socks that may get lost or caught in the filter. Make sure you do up the hooks on bras and do up zips and buttons before turning clothes inside out to further reduce the chance of any damage to it or other items in the load.

#85
SORT BY COLOUR – AND FILL YOUR MACHINE

Please don't solely rely on a colour catcher sheet. It's better to wait until you have enough whites, brights or darks before putting a wash on. Even if you seemingly get away with it, your colours will fade over time and your whites will dim to grey. It's also best to wait until you have enough clothes to fill the drum (although some machines have settings for a half load). This means fewer washes and less energy used.

#86
COOL YOUR WASH

Many people believe they won't get as effective a clean if they switch to a 30°C (85°F) wash. In actual fact, the power of the clean is only fractionally reduced while the shift from 40°C (105°F) to 30°C (85°F) can halve the energy used and therefore the cost. In the UK, it's now mandatory to display a 20°C (65°F) option on washing machines, such is the energy saving. Reducing the temperature will help both your wallet and the planet, and it's safer for your clothes, too. Dyes are less likely to run or fade; shrinking is less likely to occur.

#87
WASH BY HAND

Woollen and delicate items like lace will last much, much longer if they're treated to a bubble bath rather than thrown in the machine, even on the gentlest cycle – so roll up those sleeves. Hand-washing will help prevent your woollens from pilling/bobbling and felting; stop lace picking up unwanted colour; and guard against delicate fabrics snagging on buttons, hooks and zips. Run a sink full of warm water and dissolve a detergent specifically for delicates or a mild soap. Soak your clothes for anything up to a couple of hours. Empty the sink and fill with cold fresh water. Swish your clothes in the clean water to get the soap out and repeat the rinse stage two more times to get rid of any remaining soap. Do not wring out your woollens! It will misshape them. Instead, after giving them a light squeeze, roll them up in a clean towel to remove excess water and then leave to dry flat.

#88
CONSIDER BIO VS NON-BIO

Here's a distinction that many of us have probably never given a second thought to. Biological detergents contain enzymes to tackle bacteria whereas non-bio doesn't. This means that you may get cleaner results from a bio detergent at lower temperatures, whereas a non-bio is kinder to babies and those with sensitive skin.

The good news is that there are many eco alternatives for both out there. Whichever your preference (now that we know what the difference is and can have a preference!), brands like Ecover have you covered. The reason that even their bio products are kinder to the planet is because of lower levels of toxicity released with the waste water compared to other detergents. Ecover's packaging is also recycled and recyclable. Other eco-friendly products include a range tailored to different fabrics by the Clothes Doctor, each numbered and contained in its own snazzy aluminium bottle, and Tru Earth's Eco-Strips.

TOP TIP: Now that you're happily hand-washing your delicates, remember that the enzymes in biological detergent actually eat away at wools and silks – so never use it on these, even if you're desperate.

#89
DITCH THE DETERGENT

Not as radical an option as it sounds. The tried and tested ecoegg does a surprisingly effective job of cleaning using nothing but minerals to lift dirt. It leaves no residue and is by far the most affordable and least environmentally damaging of options for cleaning your clothes. This innovative little product is also hypoallergenic and cost-effective.

Some people also swear by soap nuts. The dried shells of *Sapindus mukorossi* (aka the soapberry tree) are natural, compostable and organic. Saponin, a soap-like foam, is naturally released when the shells are shaken in water, but it can be advisable to add some other natural cleaning agents like bicarbonate of soda as well as some white vinegar in the fabric softener compartment for the best results.

#90
GIVE UP THE TUMBLE DRYER

Tumble drying is undeniably convenient but it's really not the best thing for our clothes. It can cause shrinking at double the rate of air drying as well as colour fading. Bear in mind that natural and synthetic fabrics have different drying times, so they shouldn't all be chucked in together, and some care labels advise bypassing the tumble dryer altogether.

Line drying is far better for the fabric and uses no energy other than your own. Use an indoor rack or, if you have the space and the weather permits, an outdoor rotary or washing line. The fresh air and sunshine leave an inimitable smell and the sun has a natural bleaching effect, not to mention the antibacterial qualities of UV light. You don't need harsh, ecologically disastrous chemicals to kill odours and bacteria, just a sunny day.

#91
IF YOU CAN'T, MAKE IT MORE EFFICIENT

If time won't allow for air drying, there are ways that you can make your tumble dryer more efficient so that it won't use as much energy. Good news for your electricity bills as well as the planet.

- Make sure your clothes are not dripping wet. Put them on another spin cycle if they are.

- Give each item a shake before placing in the drum.

- Invest in some tumble dryer balls. Tennis balls in a sock, felted wool balls, or those spiky numbers that look like dog toys will soften clothes and reduce drying time and static.

- Use only low temperatures to avoid shrinking accidents.

- Empty the lint tray after every cycle to maintain efficiency.

#92
HANG UP THE IRON

The heat of ironing relaxes the fibres in the fabric of your clothes, making them easier to smooth out, but that heat can cause damage – particularly if you've got the iron set to a temperature that's too-high. Consider investing in a steamer to remove the wrinkles instead. If you've worn something the day before that needs the creases knocked out of it, take it into the bathroom with you and hang it up while you have your steamy shower. The heat of the steam combined with the weight of the garment should ease the creases out. Two jobs in one! And if you give items a good shake when they come out of the wash, they may not need ironing at all.

#93
DRY CLEANING AND THE HAND-WASH GAMBLE

Dry cleaning is not actually dry, it just uses a petroleum solvent instead of water. Health-wise, perchloroethylene aka PERC (the chemical used) is potentially carcinogenic, while environmentally it can add to air pollution and is harmful to aquatic life. The one saving grace is that, unlike water, it can be reused. However, the waste residue, still containing some PERC, needs to be disposed of as hazardous material and, like so much of our waste, is often incinerated. So-called green dry cleaners often use liquid CO_2 instead, which is significantly less toxic.

Try and limit the number of items that you dry clean. Spot clean, spritz and air as much as possible instead. It's also worth noting that sometimes manufacturers label clothes as dry clean only to cover their backs against any washing accidents. Use your common sense to judge whether it could in fact survive a cold hand-wash instead of a trip to the dry cleaner.

#94
INVEST IN SOME LONGEVITY TOOLS

There are a couple of must-have items to keep your clothes looking good as new. Firstly, get a cashmere comb, used to remove bobbles. When shorter fibres meet friction, bobbles form. These can easily be shaved off using a cashmere comb, or even a razor. Lint rollers are another must, especially if you have pets. It's amazing what de-fuzzing can do to make an outfit look as good as new!

#95
MOTH REPELLENTS

Clothes moths' sole purpose in life is to make fashion-lovers miserable. They sneak into warm dark places to lay their eggs – and when these eggs hatch, the larvae munch their way through whatever's around them. Usually a beloved cashmere jumper. To combat these evil little critters:

- Take out and shake out all of your clothes frequently, especially woollens.

- Hold things up to the light. Like vampires, clothes moths cannot abide light.

- Make sure anything stored away is clean; they are particularly drawn to any food remnants.

- Wash any infested pieces and surrounding items and clean the area around them (they can lay eggs in the dust in your wardrobe, too).

- When the items are fully dry, wrap in plastic and stick in your freezer for two weeks or more to kill the eggs.

- Use moth-repelling cedar wood or lavender in your drawers.

- Make sure your seasonal storage is moth-proof.

TOP TIP: Lavender bags are another great upcycling project for scraps of fabric and will keep those moths at bay. And if your woollens have taken a munching, see Tip 99 for darning pointers.

#96
REINFORCE

We can't consider repair without first thinking about the origin of the damage. Is it pesky nibblers? Thinning of the elbows, knees, heels, toes and other hard-wearing areas? Or a rogue six-year-old with a pair of scissors? Whatever the cause, prevention is better than cure. We've talked about pests and, sadly, the six-year-old can't always be anticipated, but when it comes to wear, we can catch it in its early stages, saving more significant mending effort later down the line. This is "a stitch in time saves nine" in action.

If an area is looking a little thin, a quick and easy thing to do to reinforce it is to use a piece of fusible interfacing. This is available in most haberdashers in black and white and can be cut to size and ironed onto the inside of the weak area. For thinning knitwear, try a duplicate stitch (a kind of darning or decorative stitch that imitates the look of knitting), which is also a great way to add pattern and individuality to your knits.

#97
SEW ON A BUTTON

One of the simplest repairs is one that only 73% of people feel confident doing, according to WRAP. If you have an item that hasn't been worn simply because it's missing a button, there's no time like the present to lift it off the repair pile, take a needle and thread and get to it. Many modern sewing machines also have the technology to sew a button on, but you need nothing more fancy than a replacement button, a needle and thread and a matchstick or toothpick.

1   Thread your needle, knot your thread, pop your button in place and bring your needle from the back of the fabric and through one of the holes on your button.

2   Now lay the matchstick or toothpick across the top of the button and sew back down through another hole on the button and the fabric.

3   Repeat until you've stitched through each of the holes a few times.

4   Remove the matchstick or toothpick and draw the needle through the button but not the fabric.

5   Wrap the thread around the threads between button and fabric a few times, knot in place and draw your needle through the back of the fabric to knot to the beginning of the thread.

6   Snip threads and pat yourself on the back for a job well done. Go hunting for other missing buttons.

#98
FIX A ZIP

A broken zip is not the garment death sentence it may seem. Invest in a zip of the same length as the one that needs replacing. Use a seam ripper to remove the old zip, taking note (photos can help) of how it was inserted. Turn your item inside out and line up your zip, face down. Pin into place on either side of the zip opening, making sure the fabric and zip are lying as flat as possible. You may want to tack, or baste (temporarily stitch), the zip in place at this stage before turning your item back the right way round. Most sewing machines come with a foot specifically for sewing zips; it allows you to get your stitches nice and close to the edge of the fabric without bumping into the teeth of the zip. Using the zip foot, sew down one side of the zip, across the bottom, and up the other side. Snip off any loose threads before taking your new zip for a spin.

#99
LEARN TO DARN

Darning is a slightly more advanced way to repair a hole or tear, and is best used on knitted fabrics. You fill the hole by interweaving yarn rather than by using another piece of material. The key is to match the thickness of the yarn you choose to mend with the thickness of the fibre in the garment and to make sure your tension isn't too tight. You can use an embroidery hoop to stabilize the area you're about to darn, or a darning egg or mushroom if it's a smaller item.

Now you're ready to begin:

1   Start below the damaged area, as wide of the hole as your patience will allow because the weakest area of the mend is where the stitches meet the hole. The wider you go with your stitches, the more secure it will be.

2   Leaving a long tail to sew in at the end, sew a running stitch in a brickwork pattern (Row 1: over under, over under; Row 2: under over, under over).

3   When you reach the hole, simply jump across to the other side, leaving a strand that bridges the gap, and continue in your brickwork pattern.

4   Continue until you've sewn a few rows beyond the top of the hole.

5   Turn your work 90 degrees and sew a running stitch that goes over each under, and under each over, of your horizontal rows.

6   Instead of jumping the hole, weave under and over the strands to create a lattice.

7   Once you've worked across all of the stitches, sew in your ends and admire your handiwork!

TOP TIP: Experiment using different colours to get a tartan effect and working on the right and wrong sides of your garment.

#100
LEARN TO PATCH

Patching works best on woven fabrics (as opposed to knitted fabrics) and can be as invisible or celebrated as you like. You will need a scrap of robust fabric, slightly larger than the rip or hole you are fixing, a few pins and a needle and thread. It can be wise to sew a zigzag stitch around the edge of your patch to stop it from fraying or you can fold the edges under but this will make a slightly bulkier mend.

Place your patch on either the front or back of your item, covering the damaged area, and pin it into place. Using a needle and thread or sewing machine, sew back and forth over the entire patch. This will hold the patch in place and secure the rip.

You can experiment with sewing around the edge of the hole and/or the edge of the patch or even try some sashiko patterns, as described in Tip 31. Oh, and there are always iron-on patches – not just brown ovals for geography teachers' elbows but in a whole range of embroidered designs!

TOP TIP: Pinning your patch to the wrong side of the item will be more discreet (if that's what you're after), as will matching the colours of the patch and your thread to the piece you're mending.

CONCLUSION

Thank you for coming on this journey. Along the way, you have hopefully found a fresh sense of your own style, learned new crafts and been inspired to make changes in the way you use and shop for your clothes. This is just the beginning of the process. Now that you've made a commitment to slow fashion, try giving yourself a larger end goal: put aside the money that you might have once spent on fast fashion to save up for a high-quality piece that you really need and will treasure.

We can learn a lot from the ways that things were done in the past, and when we combine that thinking with the technology of the present, we can create a more sustainable future together. Next time someone compliments you on your outfit, open up the conversation. Talk about the changes you're making and why you're making them. It certainly makes for a more interesting story than "It was on sale".

INDEX

RESOURCES

Organizations:

WRAP

Fashion Revolution

Eco-Age

Common Objective

The Sustainable Angle

Sustainable Fashion Collective

The Sustainable Fashion Forum

Craftivist Collective

Books:

Wardrobe Crisis: How We Went from Sunday Best to Fast Fashion – Clare Press

Fashion Ethics – Sue Thomas

Slow Fashion: Aesthetics Meets Ethics – Safia Minney

To Die For: Is Fashion Wearing Out the World? – Lucy Siegle

A Selection of Sustainable Brands:

Socko

Henri London

Ottowin Footwear

Gung Ho

People Tree

Po_Zu

Pure Waste

Bambooka Sunglasses

Y.O.U Underwear

Miss Crofton

Rapanui

Hiut Denim

Menesthò